Professor Speaks

Poetry

The inner thoughts of a strong, saved Black man

Jumanne B. Bradford

Writing is Great!

ProfXs.h.o.n. Works Publishing, Inc.
Lanham, Maryland

ProfXs.h.o.n. Works Publishing, Inc.
P.O. Box 791
Lanham, MD 20703
Website: www.profxshonworks.biz

Printed in the United States of America
Lulu.com, Inc
for Profxs.h.o.n. Works, Inc.
Contact: profxshon@yahoo.com

Library of Congress Cataloging-in-Publication
Data

ISBN
978-0-6151-9407-3

Dedication

It is at a time like this where I wish that I could be totally transparent. It is hard to see between the lines on paper. It is often difficult to find purple passion or red desire from pages of black and white. Understand that all that I do is for the love of Christ and for the love of the treasures in my life: Brittany, Zyon, and Autumn.

If you write it...

They will read.

A continuation of the thoughts in my dome.

Prof06
© 2008

I.

Poetry for me has been very therapeutic. It is able to calm my nerves and steady my soul. It is an aid that works in conjunction with prayer and praise unto the Lord. When I don't write, I have neglected an outlet that works to give me peace. Everyone has something that relaxes them and calms them, but it could be hard to stick with it because the devil does not want you to be at peace in your life. It is interesting because I have had this book completed some time ago in my mind, heart and soul, but I have not written a thing. Life just got an airtight grip on me and was not trying to let up. It was not like I was living in the world and forgot about my talents or forgot about God. It was His work that I was busy doing, so I know that I was not permitted to complete this book until now. The door has swung open wide and now it is time for me to step through.

This book is not just another project for me. Like the rest, it is special and has its own uniqueness and flavor. Some poems in this book will just blow your mind. Some may leave you confused or walking on a tight rope between worldly reality and spiritual reality. I bet you did not know that there could be a difference. My first book, ***Just My Thoughts*** was a mild look into my world and how I saw it for 20 years of my life. I don't want things to be a secret, but a testimony of how I lived in the past and how I am living now. I am not perfect and I still make mistakes, but I take responsibility for all that I do, both good and bad. This is the difference between so many and myself. I am willing to take the hit if I have messed up. I just remember that no matter what, no one here has the power or the right to judge me. I answer to my Father and if He can forgive me by looking at the blood of His Son that covers me, then I am saved.

In ***Professor Speaks***, I am befriending the lonely people who see the world as an evil place, but a place that has a lot of love and goodness in it. I am talking to those that want desperately to make change in their lives and the lives of the ones that they love, but don't seem to have a voice to do it. We can stand firm together. We can form bonds that will help us to cope and to get us through every day life. Because if you know like I do, when we chose to pick up our own cross and to follow Christ, we have become the number 1 targets of satan. It is not enough to just talk about doing things. We can pray all that we want, but God spurs us to action. Our faith produces works not the other way around. Works could never produce faith. My question to you, is what are you working for and what do you have faith in? My poems are looking at both sides of the spectrum. You cannot believe in something and have never questioned its validity or why you are doing the things that you do as you live a life according to certain beliefs.

Well, I believe in God, love, education, heritage, civil rights, and humanitarianism/evangelism. I have a passion for

Youth Ministry and when I am working with children, my fire burns deep. Every child is special. My thoughts are constantly on them and my prayers with them because I made a choice to fill my life with their lives. As a long distance dad, God knew what would help to fill the void that I have for my own. The children that I interact with every day could NEVER replace my treasures, but being a part of other young lives is what keeps me functioning every day. There is tranquility when I am looking into eyes that completely trust me and look up to me. I am a direct link to Christ for many of them, but I tell them that even I make mistakes. We all can be heroes without being perfect. It is not so much what we do, but how we conduct ourselves and prove to others that we belong to a higher power and we are not afraid to exercise the resiliency and peace that He affords us.

What I want to see is a million children with each of my books in their hands. I want them to know that there is someone out there that understands what they have to deal with. A person that understands that they too need a voice and a way to express themselves. This book is about finding that outlet and expressing it until you can't express it any more. We can all speak in more ways than just with our mouths. It is crucial that you pick up this vital revelation. My way is a pen and paper or a computer screen. I am in my

IV.

element when I can express myself in complete thought without being interrupted. This is my peace. Allow this book to help you find yours.

When you go into your Hiding place,

Do you find God?

Jesus Come

I have believed in you my
entire life
I have endured pain on your behalf
But it has been my just duty
5   I could never repay what you have done for me
I am tempted to be selfish and to focus on my
own pain
My heart skips a beat when I reflect on the shame
Too many times, I have not measured up
10   Still wanting to be like You and follow in Your
steps
Many doubt You and some say You did not exist
Praying for You to prove them wrong
Desiring to bask in Your glory
15   Your return will fill me with the greatest happiness
A joy that I am sure I cannot comprehend
Tired of hell on earth
I want to live in heaven
My stairways have been marred by
20   disappointment
My grip is fair as I hold on to You
I stand not on my own two feet
But on the shoulders of You
Who always seems to give my life plenty of
25   meaning
Outstretched arms, I long for Your touch
This is my prayer
My display of love
In You it is abundant
30   My mind just can't handle the punishment.

1

A Peace

Thinking that you can patch this hole
In my heart
Searching for something
A certain thing that is built
5   Out of faith
Wanting to find a new treasure
An angelic figure
That causes sunshine
To be born inside
10   Power released in the collision
Of pure souls
Soul mates can establish
A new
Improved path
15   The journey is long
Patience is strong
Walking in these footprints
Singing my song...

O' Lord

Omnipotence
The all seeing eye of the Father
Creation allure
Salvation pure
5 Finding you is always easy
Familiar with my sins
Cleansing the sheep from within
The measuring stick of goats
Is plenty
10 Forgiveness through mercy
Is how you repay sincere loyalty
My God
O' Lord
Magnificent is Your name
15 Commandments of love and bloodshed
Anoints the heads of your chosen people
The suffering of your Lamb
Was necessary
He who is without blemish
20 Carried the burdened cross
Heavy laden
Sin-filled
Grief stricken
Master over all iniquity
25 Jesus was pure
Honor be to the Father
The Son
And The Holy Spirit
On this day
30 Our souls are resurrected
Out of the mire of turmoil
And corruption
The shackles of sin
Are loosed

Prof06
© 2008

3.

35   Because we believe!
Accustomed to your grace
Thankful for your patience
The Messiah sits at the right hand
Of The Father
40   In His Holy Temple
Humility and a light yoke
Exist.

Each step He takes reminds me of a time of
sandals, straps, and donkeys
The measure of His will was endless
The love in His heart was infinite
5   The Covenant He kept because He was pure
Without blemish and sinless
This King of kings wears the garments of royalty
Arriving home
He could have kicked up His feet
10   His work for us was finished
But He still continued to be about
His Father's business
Having endured the strife and pain of our sins
God judged this Man according to the world
15   In which He had to conquer and live in
As the Son of God
He was the Lamb that Mary had
The sacrifice that covers all with His blood
But you must know Him
20   The gateway to heaven
Goes through this Saint of saints
In the death of this Patron
We are granted life through grace and mercy

25   Did you hear His last words?
Mary had a little lamb
And this Lamb had 12 brothers
And a world to shed His blood for
He does not represent spiritual deadness
30   But spiritual life
Even amongst those who have been dead
A long time because they know not how to forgive
A thief amongst us is presented with a choice
Love God and your neighbor

Prof06
© 2008

35 Or love that worldly voice
For the righteous
Wisdom is the decision
To care for others with your works
And God's will
40 Bringing people closer to God with the sword
On the breastplate of righteousness
Is the golden seal
For His sake
We are willing to give our lives
45 To achieve a promise that is eternal
Confess your sins
Acknowledge His blood
And love the life that was given
To spare yours
50 This is the measure of God's love.

Open the floodgates
It is time, finally!
Come this far by faith
Down
5   A pick me up
Leaning on the Lord
The victory is already won
In it there can be no weariness
The fame
10   The riches
The favor
The righteousness
But not how you think
This story has never been told
15   The His-story of the book of Life
For J.U.M.A.N.N.E. has not yet been written
It is still on the draft board
Too busy doing the will of the Lord
To stop now
20   If one be lost
Allow that one
To find your servant
In the wilderness of life
There exists thick brush
25   Lights are strategically placed in the world
To light/illuminate the pathway.

Prof06
© 2008

My First Psalm

The breastplate of righteousness has taken some
buckshots
No weapon has yet to penetrate my heart
But the attacks are coming too close
5   My mind grapples around what you want from me
Is my death desired to cause change?
Or am I to live in constant loneliness?
Not to know the touch of love
But to live in excruciating pain
10   The flood waters have drowned the ark of my
dreams
They struggle to swim, float
Throwing life preservers to rescue them
All I can do, it seems
15   No pride, just begging you for mercy
I can't accept gifts that I have not earned
Lessons learned through much controversy
It is not enough for me to love and love again
I am afraid to allow such matters to take me again
20   My spirit lags behind a world that my body just
can't catch up with
If I continue to cry alone
Will you continue to catch my tears?
It is proof that my life still rests in your hands
25   I thank you.

Prof06
© 2008

Shivering
Discontent
Disconnected
Feeling like a beast
A vagrant
A dog
Out in the cold
Not feeling too concerned
With the politics of the world
Just thinking about that next meal
Wondering about when
The luxury of "heat"
Might come into your life
The "hawk" is deadly
Able to flush away dreams
Dust down hopes
Freeze desires
What about a dream deferred?
If there are no dreams to be had
Only nightmares
Being the recipient
Of less than fortunate causes.

Blessings are counted
1,2,3…
By those that have
But they have forgotten
So this is wishful thinking
Marking territory
Making deals
Caressing possessions that aren't even there's
Trying to fit in
What never really made since
In the still of the dawn

Prof06
© 2008

9.

35   Another soul is lost
So many people of God
Claim to have another's back
Let's do the math...
How many soup kitchens have you visited?r
40   How many women's shelters are still marred
With the tormented cries of children?
How many walks have you participated in?
How many charities have you given to?
When was the last time you gave a $1 to that man
45   And told him he did not have to wash your
windows
Shine your shoes
Or give you a stolen newsletter or newspaper?
Are you human?
50   Did you stop and talk to the old man
That just wanted a little bit of your time?
He just needed a friend
For a moment
How many of us allow our female loved ones
55   To accept welfare
But not help or sound advice?

Again we must pray for our sins
Again we must pray for our neglect
60   Again we must pray for not doing our part
Of God's greatest commandment
Again we must pray because we have not shown
Much LOVE.

65

Positive outlook
Has turned out to be a trick in the dark
Inviting and enticing
But eventually a rug pulled from underneath
5   It is not just society
That buries dreams you know.

Emptying your pockets sometime means

Pulling out lint and tissue paper beads

Bills stacked high

Unable to see the sunshine through the clouds

5 A mountain of problems

Surrounded by a sea of dismay

The brick wall of unfairness looms

In the very path of righteousness

Its purpose is your demise and doom

10 Still you find a way

Still you stand tall under the heavens

Still you choose to honor the Most High

And true living God

Your happiness is not based on the ups and

15 downs

Of this life, but on the promise of the next

Each day you are given

Means that there is another opportunity

A chance to do the right thing

20 A chance to correct a mistake

A reason to not forget

That the air we breath, the food we eat, the
clothes on our backs

Are all gifts through grace

25 With the Son being the ultimate gift

Prof06

© 2008

Connecting us through faith to salvation
This is the reason we give thanks
On this occasion of Thanksgiving.

30

13.

Lord of Lords

There are those that would like
To steal my faith
To allow it would place my soul
In a guillotine
5   Severing any possibility of life
Any chance at redemption
The battle is won
Your blood shed solidifies
The presence of salvation
10   In my life
But what about the war?
There are many that doubt you
Plenty that claim of your false existence
Wanting to curse the heathen
15   Nonbeliever o' plenty
Be away with you
But I must remember my purpose
To pray for those without a clue
For those enemies that forsake thee
20   Forgiveness is theirs through my heart
Believing that the power of grace
And mercy
Travels through me as Your servant
My Psalms to you are pure
25   The tell tale signs of my Proverbs
Can be a leading testament
Or a beacon of light
The Revelation of a fallen saint
Works wonders to reveal
30   The holiness and sinful nature
Of man
Praise be unto the Most High
The thankful nature of Your children
Is plentiful

Prof06
© 2008

14.

35

Prayer and supplication for those
Marred by unbelief
Amen.

Deep, deep, deep, deep
Down
There "FORGIVENESS" lies
It is shiny and smiling
5   Wrapped in a halo
Calling for it to be taken up
And given
It resides in all of us
But sits in a different place within
10   It is centered in love
Always fights hate
Has the key to the door
Of future happiness
And always speaks to our subconscious mind
15   If we are righteous or strive to be
It beats our flesh into submission
It wipes away grudges
And heals the pain
It is rooted in joy
20   And given as a blessing
The beautiful thing about it
Is that it can be manifested
Without measure
A lot has the same effect as a little
25   Because it is always pure and truthful
You can never really ask for it
In the hearts of us all
It is either given or not
If Christ be in us
30   Then it is never a hard decision
Against anger
It will always win
The great thing about forgiveness is that
Even in the depths of our soul

16.

35
It will always
Eventually
Reach the surface of who we are
As Christians
Forgive now
40
Forgive forever
And ever

Amen.

The Reason We Commune

The dirt road to destruction is wide and dusty

The pain of suffering is as prevalent as the neigh
cries

In a barren land

So much strife

So much disdain

Few have the nerve to stand against evil

Fiery darts piercing flesh

Since some were too afraid to bear armor

Lack of faith brought us here

Jesus no longer walks in the hearts of those

Who for a short time

Claimed to believe

Ye of little faith

Will soon to be ye of no faith

How will you survive then?

By the mark of the beast?

If Christ is death

Then prepare me for the guillotine

But in physical death

Life is gained

Prof06

© **2008**

18.

The Reason We Commune

The flesh may bear the scars of the wicked
While the inner man is unbruised and untouched
Therefore Christ is life
The Lamb of God
30   Savior of all who call upon His name
The knees of the true believer
Have been scarred
Through constant prayer
No trial shall remove His name from these lips
35   By His power we stand
By His power we live
In the folds of the Father's grace
We shall eternally stay.

40   Oh, Father
Oh, Brother
Oh, Savior
Oh, Comforter
Oh, Protector
45   As we receive your body and blood today
Continue to fill us to the brim
With the will of the Father
The Love of the Son
As manifested by the Holy Spirit
50   Amen.

Prof06

© 2008

19.

It is ok to laugh and say Amen at the same time.

New York clean money
Jordans
Make high tops chillin'
White laces
5   Jump feelin'
Outfit tight
Run sneakers
Ballin' clean
Low tops
10   Why sweat?
Skip
Jam
Fly
Dirty sneakers.

If you bunch up my thoughts it looks a little like
this everything is running 2gether where are the
breaks?! the thoughts are all bunched together
no sequence no punctuation where in the world
5   are the capital letters oops was that a question or
an answer do you ever have days like this

                 what is up and what is down

10

15

can you even tell where I
am coming from
someone stop me getting
up everyday to push
through the invisible
muck and mire knowing
that you did not put it
there tell me something
do you even care

the shadows creep up sometimes making
20   life a complete living hell does this make you
insane to think like this no thoughts just get
jumbled up sometimes searching for answers that
God only knows to be true He talks to me does he
talk to you have you caught my meaning yet then
25   we must go further the red lights and the green
lights are only in place to confuse you because
everything is just yellow life is a series of yellows
caution tape police tape construction tape or
maybe that is orange but it is bright enough to get
30   your attention to slow you down to make you
think some more and to get more thought jumbled
and crammed into your tiny little 1% locker that
you can use in your brain my my how much you
know only to have someone to try and brainwash

Prof06
© 2008

35 you and to take it all away funny how some
people work to keep you down sometimes it is a
pile on of folks and circumstances but the mind
never stops taking in information if we don't
process it fast enough it ends up being a logjam
40 like this

when we want things done sometimes we have to do them ourselves it is scary like that the disappointments and the failures come together to prove one thing you know what that is that we need Jesus it is more than just a saying it is

reality

good old fashioned reality can you dig it I liked to
be understood and liked it makes me all bubbly
55 inside but my thoughts would make me unpopular
just like everyone else we think things that we
shouldn't and it is not because we want to
sometimes we are caught off guard by human
nature everyone has this problem we all need
60 prayer because these thoughts want to take a
mind of their own they want to plant seedlings of
sin and unrighteousness so glad that someone told
me a long time ago that repentance can be your
best friend it keeps you connected to the Savior
65 the truth is that those jumbled thoughts lessen in
Him. The negativity lessens in Him. Because He
told me that His yoke was light
        And he told me this in an intimate conversation

Prof06
© 2008

P

After reading His word
70 He can be the center of your life
That adds poetic bliss
Putting structure and discipline
In places that they seem to just fit
Perfectly
75 No more jumbled thoughts
No more streaks and stretchmarks
Left by problems that just won't go away
A jammed mind is a tool of satan
We must be very careful to recognize
80 The fact that he will never stop
Until Jesus comes again
Be prepared
And beware of the jumbled mind
It leads to all kinds of unsavory unmentionables
85 I don't know about you
But I don't like fiery darts
Armor of God
Do your thing!

90

Prof06
© **2008**

GPs Are Very Special

Grandparent's Day Poem
Dedicated by the 4th Grade and 3rd Dimension

You bring us lots of joy
5   Your love is measured in the gifts that you give
Your love is in great supply
And we cling to you for it
The long nights with you
Turned into sunny days around you
10   You cared for us when we were sick and down
With you everyday is thanksgiving
We thank God for the light that shines in our lives
Our thoughts are always on you
We love mom and dad
15   But there is something about our GPs
That make us forever glad
We will continue to pray for your blessings
Your love reflects the wisdom that you give
In your arms, we feel special every day
20   We salute you because nothing can break our ties
We honored you yesterday
Will honor you tomorrow
But there is a lifetime in this day.

25   GPs are as strong as oaks
You stand for righteousness
We are nurtured by the roots of your love
When we see you, a great sense of joy comes in
our hearts
30   You are a staple of our family tree
Through you we see our ancestors
The words from your mouths lift our spirits
Because of you, I am growing
Into a wonderful person

Prof06
© **2008**

25.

35   Your teachings are drops of strength in our
buckets of life
Our hearts are filled with Jesus, but your place is
also secure
When we close our eyes at night, we have visions
40   of you and all that you do
The moon could not shine brighter than the
twinkling stars in your eyes.

You are a great gift that God gave us
45   You are like a thousand pearls
When we have no one to play with, you are there
We love you in many ways
And that is why we say...
Happy GPs Day!

50

Prof06
© **2008**

Suddenly confronted to make a choice
Choosing to pray above all other things
Those around me think it strange
They are of the world
5 To display Christian behavior
Is not to seek applause
No favor sought
Only the acknowledgement of my Lord
Is wanted and can't be bought
10 Some things are just not a mystery
Eyes closed
Visions of the Lord brings light
Making an impossible decision
Easier
15 His calmness flushes the situation
Things become lighter
The heaviness is lifted
Suddenly a voice penetrates the silence
I open my eyes
20 To a slew of people staring at me
In disgust
As the lady at my favorite sandwich joint
Asks again for the 3rd time
"White or Wheat?"
25 Aren't you glad that God is everywhere?

What I desire to do is simple
I love to write
I love the prose of a situation
I love the similes as opposed to similarities
5   The metaphors of the metaphysical
Morphing words into image-producing
Sentences
When I write, I don't have to speak
I can scream on paper
10   Allow my voice to chime in any meter
I don't struggle at this
It is what I love to do.

When Life Just Plain Stinks!

Prof06
© 2008

The best way to write is to braindump and brainstorm. When we have a lot on our minds, it is better to get things out of it and off of it. The expression, "Getting things off of my chest" cannot compare to the weight that you have on your brain. When you dump, you are not being creative at all, at least not yet. It is about releasing things that are causing you great anguish and you are unable to move on to the next task or the next moment or the next project because you are still battling with certain things on your mind. Everything that weighs on us is not bad or negative. We have life changing decisions that are for the greater good, yet we have to be wise about all decisions that we make in life. The best way to dump is to put things down on paper. Unload your brain onto that paper. Use words, phrases, sentences, fragments, poems and short paragraphs. The best part about it is that you get to write it any way that you want. Write upside down if that is how you are feeling. These are excellent private moments that we can have with ourselves. Pastor Carlton Burns, Sr. and Minister Christopher Tate both have something in common. Not only are they very close to me, but they both agree that having a hiding place to commune with God is essential for healthy living. Your hiding place is where you should feel comfortable and at peace. This is where you get those things out of your brain. When the two strategies work together it allows for space in your mind for you to hear the voice of the Lord.

Prof06
© 2008

Now you are starting to get the picture. When we need to create room in our minds to make the best choices, to hear the voice of God and to contemplate and understand life's offerings, we have to make some room! Understand that most human beings have one thing in common and that is the fact that we are able to use about 1% of our brains for intelligence. Now before you jump off of the deep end, understand that that is more than enough space for us to be near geniuses. In fact, the ones that are able to operate above the 1% are those that we label geniuses. This is just further evidence that God is in control. But even with this ability, the masters of thought have to write things down and think about them just like the rest of us. Once your mind has room to move around new thoughts, you are able to then begin the art of brainstorming.

Brainstorming is easier because it can be done with more thought and planning without the burden of the emotions that occur in braindumping. Now your ideas can begin to take root and your creative nature is operating at full swing. You are the master of your thoughts now. You can open up the doors to many possibilities. When this phenomenon happens, many call it clearing your mind. This is true, but not too many people know how to clear their minds, therefore they fail to get to the point where they can be effective in creating new ideas through brainstorming. Again, this is a technique that required the recording of thoughts. Writers know this process very well. A good novel doesn't just come out of nowhere, it does not matter what the greatest writers tell you. It all starts with a single idea that opens up to more ideas and then once your mind is able to work at full capacity, a masterpiece is born! Poetry works in the same fashion for me. Each poem may start with an emotion, then a word, then a phrase, and it just keeps growing. This does not mean that the process is perfect and it goes in a particular order. This book has been in my mind for two years. I knew how to write it and to produce it, but I was unable to braindump until now. Yes, it is amazing! I have 2 years of material to now get out and I will do it and I will produce a work of art that I pray to be my absolute best. I want to touch more lives and change some minds with this project. If I am successful, I promise you that God will get the glory.

Now you may be wondering why I said that life just plain stinks. Well, can't you smell the stench of it now? It is horrible? You can look all around you and validate what I am saying. This is why we are called to be spiritual. This is why we have faith in Jesus Christ because no matter what, we can wake up and smell the roses each and every day all day because we are secure in where we are going. I turn my nose up at the world because it is run by the king of sin himself, the devil. Nothing that he has for me is better than what God has for me. So there are times when life just plain stinks and it is true. Christians struggle and we need to disconnect from the world at times. We falter, we fall, we stumble, we get dirty, we make mistakes, we get angry, we cry, we get frustrated, and we do the wrong thing, sometimes. Since this is not what we strive to be, then these times are temporary, so these are the moments when life can stink to high heaven, but remember that the statement is "When life just plain stinks" and not "Life stinks." If you can follow me and put it all together, this is why braindumping and brainstorming become so important. And they have to be done in an atmosphere the promote peace and serenity because these are the times that we see the most growth within ourselves and you certainly don't have to be a writer or poet to benefit from them.

The poems that make up this section go back as far as 6 years ago, but the meanings and power of the poems have helped me to vastly improve myself along the way. They would have never been possible if I had not learned how to get my thoughts down on paper.

? walking around without a clue
? sensing that life has nothing to offer
? is a sign that I may not receive my just due
? what this means is that I am crying in shame
5   ? a state of confusion with no one to blame
? how can one find wisdom when
? is all around
? haunts me day and night
? cannot run from it because it knows where you
10   hide
? does not play or say a word
? mocks you
? causes destruction of will
? decided to implode
15   ? no dreams can live in ? land
? the clueless nature of this beast is like quicksand
? says the more you struggle the more you sink
? we all live with it sometimes
? remains in silence and in speech.
20   ? is as ? does
To destroy it, I need a light bulb
(Idea).

Prof06
© **2008**

Head crack, head crack
The following is not a public announcement
But a look into the lives of so many that have
fallen beneath
5   The status quo
Cannot imagine the irregular heartbeat
Of a child terrified of an inevitable outcome
Stray lead pollutes their lives
Nothing to do with paint, but the bullets
10   Left alone and surely cry
Lifeless bodies of young daisies
Picked too soon in a dirty ghetto
A place where flowers struggle to grow
Dreams battle to stay alive
15   Commissioned only to be deferred
Militants no longer exist in this area
Too afraid of the dope man, dope man!

Silence kills
20   Displayed on the many faces that walk these
streets
So by dusk, the click clack of gats and shoddies
takes its place
The cries and the screams drown out a dismal
25   silence
Shades are drawn and elders flee
Too accustomed to the way things are
Not ready to pledge a decree
But what happened to Junior that made it out
30   Sure, he got a degree
But he had to keep it real and return to the hood
That dump that still had a strangle hold on his
heart

Prof06
© **2008**

35
Education did not quench his thirsty glutton for despair
What's wrong with him?
Disenfranchisement, ridicule?
Or the ability to not be able to find that good job
To pay off those student loans.
40

The mothers, oh yes the mothers
Hell bent on staying locked on welfare
Trifling is as trifling does
You can't blame that silly character of a man forever
45
After all you laid down with satan's law
Performed his acts of mischief
Now as you suffer, the child suffers
Swallow a pill of change
50
And refresh yourself with the effervescense of a cool mint
Success is more than a word
It is an idea formed
Followed by labor
55
So ripe fruits you will bear
Castrate the mentality of outright depression and lowliness
Worth is dominated by what you see when you look
60
Into that looking glass
The scar of failure is not a bar from happiness

Grass green, not here
Piles and patches of earth
65
Dingy brown to hot red clay
Leaves stains of exploitation and neglect

Prof06
© **2008**

37.

Not just on fabric, but on your very soul
Where thieves break in, but they cannot steal
What rightfully belongs to you
70   The plight of the negro is tied in with his
miseducation
She feels the blunt force of the billy club too
Most times with certainty, it is indirectly
History don't mean a thing, jive turkey
75   Unless you have learned something from it
Bliss ain't never been kin to ignorance
So you betta watch yo' step around here
This here is your wake up call and it won't come
again.
80

Oh, but don't fret, the whites, the browns, the
yellows and the reds
They got it bad too
The quo has drawn a distinct line in the sand
85   The bottom line is money
Not into makin' no friends
The American pie has been sliced a long time ago
If you want opportunity to knock
Then you have to show up at the door
90   Running scared is not a branch of faith
When your turn comes you take it
Procrastination is dead, no need to wait
Stir up trouble and you will live with the serpents
The ability to survive is a given
95   Firm belief is a constant struggle
But to live is to live out today
The best you possibly can
Leave tomorrow until tomorrow.

Prof06
© 2008

I know why Black men lose it
Sometimes
He is usually born of an angry Black man
He grows up abused
5   He grows up being used
What can he do but struggle
To live in a society
That wants to keep him down
He lashes out at loved ones
10   That don't believe in him
He continues down that long road
Despite being beaten
And kicked along the way
Such a man scars
15   Eventually having to deal with his own
Anger
Pain
The Black man that I speak of
Can snap and make a decision
20   That destroys his life
Or chooses to do something
That will take it
He wants to share his life
He gives all that he can
25   Even when he is down
A Black man cannot survive
On criticism alone
Without encouragement and love
He is a lost soul
30   He who live and breathes
Is me.

Prof06
© 2008

What can you do?

Hearts are won on a battlefield of unyielding
despair
The songwriter says no matter what the people
say...
5 Not true
When you are the child that battles with self
esteem
Negative
Bottom feeding on the fuel that wants to see your
10 insides implode
Masked face
Feelings turning into concrete stone
The chills of fallen possibilities no longer cause a
shudder
15 It was all good until that day
That day when this young, promising soul took his
own life
No one led this person to God
No one mentioned the blood of Jesus
20 But Fox news is telling about the blood of this teen
That was shed too soon
Common are our Black youth to be lost to violence
Even if it is self inflicted
No love for self
25 But too much love for everything else in the world
Unable to grasp it
This young soul sees life as not worthy to live
What can you do?
What can you do?
30 No one ever listened to the voice that cried from
within
Not a soul paid attention to the looks in the eyes
That were fed up with crying
In fact, they were dried out from crying too much

35   Ever been there?

It is not too late

The knowledge of the experience that one life
took

Is enough to warn you to take a different look

40   At yourself when you look into the mirror

If you can't figure out the meaning of life on your
own

Then you need help and it is there

It is nearer than you think

45   Just fall on your knees and look up

Someone is waiting on your love and your faith

The only one that will give love in return and
never let you down

Now you know the answer of what you can do.

50

Prof06
© **2008**

Pollution

Waste in the byproduct
Of our daily activities
The unmentionables that we are too happy
To get rid of
5   Things no longer needed and are put away
The items no longer of necessity
That have run amuck or astray
How can these things be decided?
To be of no consequence in our lives anew
10   We hoard these things as collectibles
Not know what an abundance of them can do
Stacking and stashing these things in one place
About as helpful as stuffing dirty clothes
In a drawer
15   At some point all things discarded
Become noticeable again
The concentrated stench
And the overbearing breakdown
Elements form the things that we used
20   Never too pleasant when they reform and combine
To create a whole new dimension
Of unbearable crap
Then the problem is bigger than imagined
When things die and things suffer
25   It must be enough
This retched habit has been going on for years
The corruption of our waters, land, ecosystems
And climates
Animals and People are at greater risk
30   The longevity of the planet depends on how well
It is treated
EPA is not enough to save us today
Recycle is done only in a few cycles
Or a few ciphers

Prof06
© 2008

35   Some care and some don't

What in the world is becoming of our hope?

Create areas of disaster relief

End the practice

Of political and economical pollution

40   Now!

Prof06
© **2008**

Alone

Many of us are alone

Walking down a road trodden

With mystery and uncertainty

The things of the world have us twisted

5   Smiles upside down

Resembling some so sin-naster

Why frown?

A gaping whole exists in the hearts of many

A void too deep

10   Too wide

To be filled by man's conventions

If you take the pulse of this deadened nation

How many folks will you find actually alive

With the love of Jesus Christ?

15   Would you find many?

Any amongst your kin?

Your friends?

Prof06
© 2008

Your spouse?

20   Our mistakes do not have to condemn our future

If you are on this road

Pump the breaks

Distance yourself from all things

Unrighteous

25   It is unfair to deny yourself

Salvation

In lue of stubborness and bitterness

Magnify the burdens that you carry

Heal through prayer and forgiveness

30   Repent to He that has the power

To make you whole again

I cannot stand for you

He has already died

I can pray for you

45.

35   My friend

                    So therefore I do without ceasing

                        It is simply all that I can do...

                    But never feel that you are alone

40   From this point forward.

Prof06
© **2008**

I am not looking for a handout
I just want to know
Where is my money?
The dream that is supposed to be
As American as apple pie
Why has it eluded me?
What gives?
It was supposed to be related
To the amount of education
That I have received
But that dollar ain't no kin to me
It runs from me like
A Biblical plague
Working ain't enough
I ask for it and people look at me sideways
Hard work lived in this vessel
But still no dice
Grinding and pushing
But not how you think
The honest living
Amounts to minimum wage
If I was living the other way
This lyrical battle would not be taking place
I would have the bling bling
Making jealous ones envy my shine
Telling kids that you too
Can be like me
Only if you are willing to do the wrong thing
And in some cases
Sell your soul
Maybe not to the devil
But there are plenty
That have the same panache
With the same deal

Prof06
© 2008

47.

35   Not to sound ungrateful

I have my life

Because for this

Some would kill

I guess

40   I just want what everyone wants

To be able to live a life of luxury

I am sorry for my lapse

Even I get caught up in the world at times

No commercial

45   Car

Object

Or Place

Could make me forget who I am

Inside

50   I just wish what every child wishes

That I could just get a pair of Jordans

Oh, and a Nintendo Wii, too.

Prof06
© 2008

<u>Too Late</u>

Those cold words
Ring so true
Sounds of shame
Echo the shards of reality
5   Shut them out
Earplugs
Headsets
Cotton
Customized devices
10

Nothing can stop what you already know
Begging won't make a difference
Pleas fall on deaf ears
The receiver of the phone hits the floor
15   A crushing blow
A loud thud
No longer a cushion for your falls
But a brick wall to knock you right back
From whence you came
20

Fate never seemed so unlucky
Sometimes the head reared
Is uglier than you can imagine
Hope is fading like quicksand
25   The branch of salvation looms
Just out of reach
Only divine intervention can save you now
Praying never seemed like the best alternative
Instantly, it is all that you have
30   Whether you use it
Is up to you.

Prof06
© **2008**

Migraine

Pulsating
Penetrating
Goosebumps going inward
Tickling your brain
5   Thunder claps, flashes of light and winds of hate
Shake and toss your grey matter
One side of the mind is dedicated to chaos
The other clings to relief
What side wins
10   Will be written all over your face
Torn
Uprooted
Just unable to function
Weathering an impossible storm
15   Gel caps, red and yellow candy
Even the powdered stuff is ineffective
What rock have you overturned?
To piss off the source of this pain
Madman
20   Madwoman
Hard to focus
Difficult to stand
Light-headed
Stuck in a mental traffic jam
25   Every single collision is a silent and deadly death
Before the dawn of its conclusion
You must endure
The Explosion.

I am still Hip-Hop!!!

Back in the day
Early
On an asphalt pavement
80's cool breeze morning
5   Wheelin'
Pop-lockin'
Spinnin'
Wavin'
Style so smooth
10   Body movements of effortless ease
Shelltoes
Black and red stripes
On a slim, flexible suit
Cardboard and portable stages
15   Small hood crowds
To large stadium venues
All showed the love for a culture
Never lost

20   The influence of your beginnings
Extends far beyond the wildest imagination
Graffiti tagged you
Artists penned you
Rappers fed on energy from you
25   Many predicted your demise
It was a fad
A short-lived punk phenomenon
Like Hip-Hop you were supposed to be...
DEAD
30   Resurrection prophesied
Cornerstone or similar to the return
Of Christ
No shame of who you are
As old as the "wheels of steel"

Prof06
© **2008**

35

As fresh as the tired cliché
"Bling, Bling"
B-Day: Honor and Respect.

Brown

Down, down, diggy, diggy, down, down
Way down to the nippity nap sack of brown
The dude in the slick corduroy jacket
With those soulful suede patches
Afro picked out nice
Round and crazy brown
With a streak of confidence
The gait was like a smooth brown sway
In the cool autumn breeze
Clickety clack
Side step, oooh!
Those shoes spit shined
Gleaming with a dark brown hue
So in tune, the man could tap dance
As he makes his way down the avenue
Catdaddy, likes his women chocolate brown
And fashionably sassy
Gliding to and fro
While dropping an occasional pound or two
The sugary vanilla brown kisses
Of several mistresses
Leaves a crooked, sly brown smile on his face
Cool as Shaft
Fly as Sly without his Family Stone
A charming prince
Holding captives with his light brown eyes
What's he driving?
Nothing but a caramel brown Cadillac
As he purrs that engine and begins to pull off
Some unknowing soul
Had a nerve to ask, "Who dat?"
Fool, that strong super cat is…
The Brown Hornet.

Mama, I Made It!

Mama, I made it!
Finally, you helped me face it
The terror of these mean streets
Tried to replace me
5   With a colder, deader version of me
Couldn't escape the traps
I am cornered
Just wanted to be free
Times like this
10   I had to rely on my Father
Not the one that you think
I don't even know who he is
Just a phantom in my imagination
My heavenly Dad is real
15   He has protected me because I believe
The reality of these mean streets
Tried to swallow me up
I did all I could to miss the potholes
The stumbling blocks of drugs, sex and guns
20   The false pride and the ineptitude
All lie in wait for my soul
I just couldn't play on his playground
You know
The red man with the pitch-fork
25   The horns
And the devious smile
He wants too much
His price is too much to pay
He required a payment
30   That I did not have the means to pay
You see
My life is not my own
So how could I give it away?

Prof06
© 2008

35 Mama always told me that I would
Do great things and never look back
I never asked for handouts
Or gifts in return
For my acts of kindness
40 I was in church
At first, against my will
But then I learned to love that fellowship thang
It was cool
I just wanted to be noticed
45 By God's people
Not by the fools running game
At the local corner store
I graduated in many ways
Not just in the school of thought
50 But also in the school of hard knocks
Excuse me if I seem too contrite for your taste
But Mama, I made it!
Despite the charm of sin
Talk of failure
55 And me being a waste
Yeah, I have heard it all
And it never stops
People are trying to hold me down now
Not able to grasp
60 The level of godly favor that I possess
A life of peace and of less stress
If you can't see it
I will just pray for you
If you believed in me
65 Then you believed in the Christ within
Because I did not do this on my own
I was chosen for greatness
Still I had to make the choice

Prof06
© **2008**

70

Mama, I made it!
Now in peace you may rest.

Mama is gone
But I kept my promise.

<u>Challenge My Style? (Never)</u>

You can't hold me
I am out the box, Fool!
That rebellious slick cat
Making my moves
5   Poppin' my locks
Breakin' in my shoes
Phunk what ya heard
I ain't got nuttin' to lose
Boombox siren
10   Asphalt smashin'
Nobody betta challenge me
In my hood
Just not happenin' on my block
Neva lost a battle yet
15   In the malls
On subway stairs
Schools
In your face
I swear
20   I will embarrass you
In front of ya girl
Top spin is just vicious
Sporting the latest styles
Since
25   **A**ll **D**ay **I D**ream **A**bout **S**pinning
The high is better than sex
I have a rep to protect
An image to uphold
They call me the King
30   The Grandmaster of this art
Nobody can fade me
Not even black has enough power
To oppress me
I am a natural figure

Prof06
© 2008

35   Born to occupy infinite space

For an infinite destiny

How can you even fathom

To be able to taste the

Fine flavor

40   Of this divine B-boy

I am in my stance

Awaiting my next challenger

Another victim...

Prof06
© 2008

Haiku

The ice brings no frost
Frigid temp of hearts now lost
The cold of winter.

Haiku

Do you Haiku, too?
More to it than meets the eye
5-7-5, right?

Fierce as tornadoes
Twisting and turning fates hand
Wind up poor in spirit.

Natural dreams squeeze
Natural possibili-
Tees into sweet thoughts.

Haiku

Come on you can try
Nature's fingertips apply
To mind and paper.

Causin' confusion
You comin' into my life
How dare you, lady?

Haiku

When the clouds hang low
Opaque features, hidden face
I hardly knew you.

Stepping in the venue
High heeled stilletoes and platforms
Afro picked out
Perfectly round
5   The striking sound of
A disco inferno
Bass boomin'
Crystal clear vocals
Of a sensual sexy singer
10   Only grown folks party here
No drama
From yo mama
Not even the one that had
Yo babies
15   Just a groovy time
Spent with classy people.

I am not political...

Or am I?

African
American
Beautiful
Creation
5 Kemet
Egyptian
Technology
Medicine
Pyramids
10 Devine
The Nile
Intelligent
Courageous
Tenacious
15 Hard Working
Godly
Wisdom
Strong
Nurturing
20 Artistic
Poetic
Song
Dance
Love
25 Desire
Worldly
Smiles
Talent
Blood
30 Tears
Struggle
Discrimination
Battle
Fight

Prof06
© 2008

35   Positive

Finding the words to describe myself comes easy

Creating an image of my people is worth while

The good and the bad are seen in our history

40   We are more than conquerors

Beyond simplicity

The synergy that we once shared has been stolen

Taken from us around the time we were

kidnapped

45   Beyond our shores of the Motherland

We were made to suffer

Our worth was taken down to the lowest peg

To believe that the bottom rung of the totem pole

is where we belong

50   Our children miss the black history that will fill

them with pride

African pride

Prof06
© **2008**

Black pride

American pride

55   This country was built on our very backs

But no one wanted to really trace our roots

We all are Kunta Kente, Marcus, Malcolm, Martin,

Sojoyner, Harriet, Madam C.J., Oprah, Mahailia,

Frederick and Lena

60   Their spirits and their very blood lives on in their

families

And in everyone that they have paved the way for

or influenced

February is not the time to blow the dust off the

65   old black history books

12 months out of every year is appropriate

Our lack of knowledge in ourselves

Creates a self loathing

And a system of beliefs fathered by other people

70   From other races

If you don't know who you are

You will never know where you are going

Silver spoons and platinum platters are not

abundant

75   In our communities

If you want success, you have to build success

And not be afraid to help others too

Give abundantly and you shall receive

The greatest command is to love

80   But your hate is shedding the blood of our men on

the streets

Your disdain for your own skin is shooting the

drugs into our veins

Filling your lungs with that smoke

85   Spoiling your liver as you drink

Crusting your nose as you snort

Prof06
© **2008**

72.

The death you bring yourself

Is the death that you bring your family

Ultimately your race

Backwards

90

Negros

make

me

sick.

73.

Musta been blind
Thinking that you were gonna get that lucky break
Please
You've been shuckin' and jivin'
5   And don't have nuttin' to sho fo it
I am tired of you backwards types
Thinkin' dat nun ov us can speak propa English
Ya tried to educate me outta an outdated book
Tryna create a new and out dated fool
10   Hatin' on me becuz of da color of my skin
Destroyin' my self worth becuz my hair iz different
Lambs wool covers that knowledge that you and
ya cohorts tried to take
All grown and educated and you can see that in
15   my walk
What can you do when Amiri Baraka still lives?
When Maya Angelou still speaks?
When Langston calls from the grave?
When Mumia rots in jail, but still has a voice?
20   You can try, but you cannot silence us all
No backstabbing, backsliding
Single-minded negro is going to stop me
Send who you want
No fool with a slave mentality can even breathe air
25   in my cipher.

Come again?
What is it that you want?
Moving to and fro
30   Plotting to devour all righteousness that you can
find
Must the movement be rekindled and marred with
corruption
At the same time?

Prof06
© 2008

35 Too many inquisitive thoughts
    Questions pile high
    To an infinite sky
    Not worried about the repercussions of what a
    worldly power can do
40 This soul is not for sale
    Creepin' on in and tryna pull me back to my roots
    But I call them weeds
    An identity that was forced onto my ancestors
    Choking their true existence
45 That used to bud like the most beautiful Nubian
    flowers
    We are returning to that
    And I know that you hate it
    Proving you wrong will be the biggest love of my
50 life
    God knows the heart that beats for a new day
    A day of love
    I have no disdain for you
    I cry out for you to just be fair
55 Before it is too late
    Too late to save yourself from a fate that the most
    brilliant mind cannot fathom
    For all of the death, the accomplishments, the
    shortcomings and the lies
60 You still remain strong
    But there is a chink in the American armor
    It is called self hatred and lust
    When you look in my face
    Do you still want to spit?
65 Hose me down?
    Unleash your ferocious dogs?
    My face is of those that hung from trees
    Strange fruit indeed

Prof06
© **2008**

But only because we were castrated, humiliated
70 and decimated against our will
All did see
Some were very glad
Others sad
You see, you are not the enemy
75 But some that live amongst you are just those
same sheep
Donning the wolf's clothing worn many times.

Controversial figures
Lead us to death sentences
Come join us
Dying to live amongst the stars
Fake saluting a government
That would rather lynch us
Bush burning
Reaganomics
Dead brain cells
Actors flipping the script
Honoring crooks with airports
You want a voice of reason
Then don't silence mine
Really you can't
Not even death could keep me from it
Color purple
Black
And blue
Jealous of not having rich culture
So fame is sought by stealing others
Foreign backstabbers
False alliances
Playing with black and brown resources
Close borders
Only to open floodgates for more
Drugs
Oil
Terrorism
Pain
Strife
Death
Hate
All the while
Tons of money to be made

Prof06
© 2008

You Can't Shut My Mouth!

Man in the mirror is a Satanist with horns
You can't twist a mind once it is pure
Truth sets some of us free
Other remain in shackles
By choice.

You Can't Shut My Mouth!

Allow me to hold your hand
Telling you of my desires to love
Love a willing soul in the naked sands
Of time
Your heart found one
Buried deep in the muck and the mire
A piece of rugged coal
Not yet a diamond
In the rough
But victim to the pressure of time and
circumstance
Believing in my worth
Not succumbing to the thoughts
Of the All Powerful
Flipping a coin to decide my fate
Not ashamed of my doubt
I was simply not ready
To accept a yearning soul
For the same things
That my soul desired
Crossing concrete jungles
Fighting principalities unseen
I deemed you my queen
Deserving the abundance of love
Born in me to give to the world
Begotten and commissioned
By God to cause changes in fates
Burying the fake
Destroying blatant hate
Desiring to be the very reflection
That stares hypocrites down
Turning murdered soldiers into martyrs
It was you that I first loved
For just being real

Prof06
© **2008**

You Can't Shut My Mouth!

Offering yourself to me
Unconditionally
Performing your wonderful art
Of self expression
I am with you.

Prof06
© 2008

You Can't Shut My Mouth!

Mix my emotions up in a bowl
Feel them raw and uncut
Yes, I am sick
I am sour with all the sweet negroes
Politicians and crooks
Ashamed to call you heroes
You are stealing from your own people
Cheating
Making babies of destruction
Absent fathers
"F" these niggas that we call our heroes
All you can do is dribble a ball
Throw a pass
And hit a rock
Forgetting about those that need your attention
Voting Rights are not rights at all
Fight for amendments and laws
Cut the B.S.
Selfish bastards
Walking on the graves of our very ancestors
I wish I could forget that I was saved
Bury you fools in your own waste
Weapons of destruction are not the guns
But your seeds that you fail to raise
Martin and Malcolm are heroes
50 don't make much since (cents)
"G" is the only letter in the alphabet
He seems to have taken time to learn
Conscious Kanye and Common
Need to form alliances that sell education
Not just hope and rhymes
Battle the establishment
Like real African soldiers
Lives on the line

Prof06
© 2008

81.

You Can't Shut My Mouth!

Too many have been raised to be cowards
Disrespecting our women
Disdain for your mothers
Creates disdain for our mothers
Follow me
A cycle repeats itself
Of itself a cycle will repeat
Not letting go
Until it is broken
Smashed
Destroyed
Instead of becoming spokes
For a wheel of oppression
Blacks need to be centers of love and commitment
Major in Jesus
Economics and Leadership
Any man can be a leader
Some are born and some are taught
Stereotypes are only prisons
For those that are too conditioned to not fight
And too conditioned to be pawns
On a chess board that is not even their own
Bill has it right
But you backwards, bootlicking, trustee negroes
Don't want to upset the real breadwinner
You bring home the scraps that the oppressor
gives you from his table
Don't poke your chest out
You take that same money and buy their products
Buy black and spend black dollars
Create a new cycle of Black love and Black unity
Make it so powerful
That greenbacks

Prof06
© 2008

82.

You Can't Shut My Mouth!

Cause America to remember the blackbacks that
created this country
America the beautiful
Is only the way she is because we built it
America is great because we made it great
Now I feel a little better
My vent is wide open.

Twisting
The knot gets tighter
A lump of spoiled beliefs
Sits inside the pit of my stomach
The juices of sin
Produces a strong acid
That erodes the lining of my throat
The words just don't come
Painful to admit a mistake
The trespass was too great to reveal
Stuck between a rock
And a hot place
Penetrating
The bottomless abyss
Touching what is sacred
Desires of the heart were bypassed
Altogether missed

Prof06
© 2008

83.

TELLING ME THAT I DON'T KNOW WHAT TO SAY
MISSING THE POINT
HURTING FEELINGS
PENNED UP FRUSTRATIONS
BUILDS UNPENETRABLE WALLS
GRACE CAN'T SAVE YOU NOW
TRYING TO ARTICULATE THE MEANING OF MY
EMOTIONS
I SEEM TO LOSE YOU EVERYTIME
TO MOTION SICKNESS
FROM SEE SAW BATTLES
LOVE GETS MASKED
UNDER A FILM OF MISUNDERSTANDINGS
DESIRES ARE SWALLOWED

Prof06
© 2008

Believe in me
Support me
Vote for me
The bottom line is always clear
5   Not seeing me as more than just 3/5^{ths}
You want my input
I am the African
Born American
That you want to use
10   To get what you want
My issues are not on your agenda
Nothing that you say
Could make me feel otherwise
Many of my ancestors have trusted
15   In your people
Only to be led to the slaughter
And the guillotine
Who could blame you for trying?
Most of you have successfully
20   Brainwashed and fleeced
Several "black" sheep
At least you recognize that we
Who are defamed
Are crucial to you election
25   You need one Black leader
One Black cause
And one Black baby
You mix them together to appear
That you have our interests at heart
30   You end up giving us bones
While you and your people
Devour a full course meal
There is no justice or honor in that
There is no God in it either

Prof06
© **2008**

35
What is real is what you do
When there are no cameras
No media
No turnout
40
No fame to be gained
Are you as polite
Forthright in your concern
Do you give aid to my people in need?
Your tax cuts have not put extra green
45
In my pockets
As you continue to use what you have taken
To build more bullets, bombs and rockets
I didn't sign up to have my money used for that
You don't speak on that
50
In fact, you probably have made millions
From taking my money and the money of millions
Like me
Trust is not an option here
Belief is not something that you are going to get
55
My divinely inspired faith only goes up towards
One
His name, nowadays you can't even say
So who is fooling who?
It is not your ways that disturb me
60
It is the fact that you constatly
Vehemently
Come after my vote
Underneath your raging
Wolf pack of lies
65
No thank you
I am not into politricks.

Prof06
© **2008**

Pale Face

One day they are going to show you
Rich and powerful
Believing that they really want your company
Secure in your pop status
5   You arranged to infiltrate the ranks
Even to the detriment of your own race
Childhood to adulthood
You managed to erase in you
What it means to be black
10   At least on the outside
It truly does not matter if you are black or white
But it matters when you start one way
End another and still lose the fight
Confusion may not be what is on your plate
15   But for those that love you
It feels like being served raw stake
Through the heart
We have supported you well into the night
And surely at daybreak
20   Please forsake us not because we claim you
In God's name for His sake
Your works have been historic
Ignoring the fact that you seem to be
The little boy who never grew up
25   Your face is now but a mask to hide your former
self
The veil and mask that you wear is unnecessary
Because we already do not know who you are
Trials and tribulations came and we still stood by
30   you
Never wanting to believe that you could do
heinous acts
Or be found to be a smooth criminal
I pray that you get your affairs in order

Prof06
©2008

87.

35   Rock the night away with adults and not with
babies
Your children need you now
The thrill is ov'er
Please sir, come back down to earth
40   Peter Pan is fictitious
Show us again the real MJ magic and worth.

P

There is nothing like family.

Even if we are crazy!!!

For the Lord, that is!

Daddy Cares

Being a dad is one of the hardest things to do
But one of the easiest to accomplish
It is so simple
You just have to be there
5   Physically
Young children
Don't care or understand
The reasons or excuses
Not being there
10   Is not being there
Physically
Never mind the gifts
The calls
The well wishes of love and kindness
15   Sorry, Daddy
You lose
If you are not there
Physically
The wonder years
20   Are those first years
No matter what you have been through
Or what you are trying to do
If you cannot be there for your children
Physically
25   You lose their respect
And their love
How can a good man hold his head up?
Knowing that his children ask questions
That go unfulfilled
30   They participate in plenty
Activities o' many
And you just get the score
Or a dry update
Sometimes pictures help

35 But it unleashes the sorrows
Of past sins and failures
That were locked away in your heart
Sure, you have forgiven yourself
But have others forgiven you
40 No bad hands dealt here
This dad accepts full responsibility
For successes as well as failures
Not too kosher when you turn things around
But still get the same results
45 Distance is all too familiar
Felt it growing up
Even when so many people were near
Some can't even fathom what that feels like
No words could unlock the plethora of emotions
50 When it comes to the thoughts of a good man's
children
They are the only ones that have a key
Dad must sit in constant silence
While life eats away at him
55 Make no mistake
It is not guilt that he feels
Just a certain despair that he cannot control
The one thing that makes him fall to his knees
No one knows the struggles of a father
60 Who must win
No rat race is hard enough
Or difficult enough to hold him down
He expects understanding and respect
But most often falls short of his expectations in
65 those areas
Not getting angry or discouraged
He forgives them for ignoring his dreams
More than wants or needs

Prof06
© 2008

A destiny of some sorts
70 He once spoke of Treasures
And how much they meant to him
It has not changed
But fear of the change in them
Fear of not hearing their voices with pleasant
75 tones
Fear of another man hearing those words
I love you, Dad
Fear that touches and hugs will be marred by the
years
80 That stand in between
Fear that my tears are just water
Marking a dying emotion
Fear that you could never love again
Because the love that you long for
85 Is missing
Cannot be replaced
And the area that it is found in is out of your reach
The joy and pain of seeing other dads raise their
children
90 It is great to see
But it is them
Dad is envious and jealous
Of the time that they get to spend
The darkside of the force
95 Tends to want to consume Dad
But his lightside
Is marked by the blood of the Savior
So Dad gravitates towards it
Not understanding why he is in this place
100 Not realizing the implications of sharing his
thoughts
It is therapy in some form

Prof06
© 2008

Not saying that he is not lost
Other Dads have suffered this same fate for years
105   Not saying that a woman can't do it
Utilize a good father when he is available
If he does not make excuses
Neither should that mother
Not knowing what a Dad should do
110   Is the biggest crime of a father.

Nevermind the cliché saying
I envisioned the time
Of football games
Playing tag and riding bikes in the sun
5   My buddy
My true playmate
A mini me
Spending time together just having fun
Walking and talking
10 Smiling and profiling
Just like me
Handsome and kind
This little chap has a heart of gold
He gets to live like I wanted to
15 I catch his tears when he cries for me
Physically, I am his Dad
But when a part
I touch him spiritually
Because he is me
20 I can't help but feel his pain
You see
Daddy has his girls
Sweet and delicate
But his Y chromosome
25 Comes from Daddy J.B.
Rough around the edges
Innocent and good
Like his sisters
He loves the Lord
30 And his parents for sure
My hardness will make him tough
My love for him seems to be just enough
Tight handshake that shows confidence
He has been raised in the right way

Prof06
© 2008

35   A testament of his maternal influence
You know it still takes two
When I saw you for the first time
You took my breath away
A son to a father
40   Is a blessing
One that brings serenity
He is my boy
Da Boy
Affectionately nicknamed
45   I am proud of him
Because his character could never bring shame
My gentle giant
My one and only son
You are still my Simba
50   And you will always be
The only one.

Prof06
© **2008**

Daddy's Girls

The pleasant smells
Sugary sweet
The birth of tiny angels
The ones that seem to speak
5   Directly to my young soul
Pretty brown eyes
Gorgeous smiles
Lively personalities
Are what make my life complete
10   In these God-given rays of sunshine
I often find peace
When the two
Lovingly wrap their arms around me
I am truly the king that I deserve to be
15   A hero in their eyes
A sinner
But one with endless possibilities
To show them what being a good man
Is all about
20   The time that we spend
Is more that priceless
It could never be measured
The worth of it is only known
By the value of heaven
25   Our walks are missed
Our talks are balm to my soul
You have healed me is ways
That you will never know
A Dad loves his children
30   From the time of conception
Until that last breath
I am buried in your memories
Today
I continue to take steps

Prof06
© 2008

35   Until we meet again

It will be very soon

My daughters

My sunshine

Your brightness

40   Is what illuminates the moon

Life is reality

More than just a movie

The silver screen got one thing right

To protect you in my duty

45   At night when you are afraid

Just imagine my arms around you

I am your comfort from God

Your shade from evil

And the absorber of your pain

50   My girls

My treasures

You have not lived life yet

Until you have seen

Daddy again.

DiONNA not DieONNA

If I think of your near miss
It creates powerful emotions
I lost a brother
Gained a sister
5   And now...YOU!
Poobie
Born at a time that was so
So special for me
Glad to have you
10   Your entrance into this world
Meant more than seeing
Those twin towers
Never thought I would see them fall
But when you fell
15   My life was truly in slow motion
Life with constant loss leaves the heart lonely
Prone to bitterness
Baby girl
So bright and full of life
20   Independent and smart
Your desire to be where the action was
Brought you to the street
It was not your time
Thankful that the speed of the car
25   Was commanded by God
In the hands of a sweet older lady
Still afraid
I feared for your life
Just as I feared for Kiki
30   There was a time when I believed
That I was to be Mom's only child
Wanting siblings
Some disappeared
Leaving me without a smile

Prof06
© 2008

35   Or explanation
Suddenly, your energy was gone
We rushed to you
And you began to cry
We all did
40   Simultaneously, we thanked God
You were still alive
Child of light
It was not your time
On a street filled with racers-by
45   Those careless drivers that despise red
Only seeing green
You were spared by swift winds of change
Your little "i" was not to become an "ie"
To this day
50   I still don't know how
You quickly descended those stairs
Fractured leg and all
I was glad to carry you
Back up those same stairs
55

As I look at you today
I am proud of your growth
Whether you remember or not
It will remain a large part of why
60   I cherish you so much.

Prof06
© **2008**

P

I Was There

(For Zakiyah)

Always
Never had to ask
Caring for you
The past made present
5   With every turn of the hand
Remembering is what counts
Reflections on how you came to be
Being a big brother is an honor
Never a burden were you to me
10   When you hurt
I hurt more
When you cried
I cried more
I know that I was tough and mean
15   At times
A boy being responsible
At all costs
Was never an easy task
So yes
20   I take pride in who you are today
I stayed by your side
Lonely nights
After long days
I never felt alone when I was with you
25   My little sister
You got on my nerves
And I was always "treatin" you
I had to leave you behind
In that are many regrets
30   But my life had to take a turn
There were just too many secrets
Harbored deep inside me
I couldn't be a chip
Because off that old block

Prof06
© **2008**

100.

I Was There

(For Zakiyah)

35
I had to leave
Never knew
If I made an impact on you
Until I saw you graduate
In some ways
40
I paved the way
Suffered
In order for you
To make your life more complete
Two siblings
45
That had a mother and a father
But something was always missing
To the best of my ability
I tried to supply it to you
I lost growing up
50
Big Brother and Big Sister flew the coup
I never wanted to do that to you
The past becomes present
Through your accident
That same eye
55
It must be special
God has allowed you to keep it
The blinds couldn't take it
Neither could the bus
I was there for it all
60
Wanting to once again
Steal your pain and make it my own
You can't blame a brother for trying
I won't like all of your choices
But they are your choices
65
And I understand
Hard head like mine
With an attitude to match
Our parents did a number on us

Prof06
© 2008

I Was There

(For Zakiyah)

But we always do our best
70   This is my ode to you
Because I have always been there
Waiting for you to need me
Ready to give advice and to share
I am always big brother
75   Ready and willing to take your pain
Only your husband should care the same
And in that there is no shame
I am glad that you are in a period of joy
Because neither one of us likes the rain.

Prof06
© 2008

102.

It always has to be
Wet, wrinkled, and satisfactory
Stuck in your mouth
What is it that makes you
5 So much like your sister and mother?
Silly thing
Cute as a button
That one extension constantly drowned
In that moist cave of darkness
10 I tried to take it
To keep it for myself
What is so tempting about it?
Tried to break you
Nothing seemed to work
15 Now the image of you
Without your classic trademark
Is inconceivable
Keep going, girl
It is a part of who you are
20 Your personality is glued to that thumb
Rest assured that you may grow out of it
And your transition will begin
Regardless of that habit
You have compiled an impressive
25 Resume' of talents and accomplishments
When you are serious
When you are performing
That thumb goes away
It disappears to only reappear later
30 But when work has to be done
It dries and gets into position
That thumb does its part
Pushes the limits
Because it knows that later

Prof06
© **2008**

35   It will submerged
                                    In all of your love and affection.

I love you, Lainey! You know that I had to mess
with you.

P

Tears are therapeutic...

It reminds us that we are human and that we have feelings.

The roughest day that I can remember
When I say "I" it does not mean "Me"
Per se
Caught in the mind of another
5   A close, but distant being
This fellow has made some things happen
And this is what I mean
Grew up hard
Without many hugs
10   Longing for attention
The boy within just wanted some love
Conversations with himself revealed
Great talent
But the talks just ended
15   With more questions than answers
Leaving him to wonder
If you really can answer yourself
Not too selfish to be a loner
But sometimes too giving to handle
20   His own problems
Too many people look at his words
And totally misunderstand
Miseducated?
No, just a Black man
25   Trapped in a distant land
For him, respect is not earned
Every move is a motive
To be compared to another
And this he does not deserve
30   Pat him on the back?
Don't you dare!!!
He still owns up to his mistakes
Without cry or despair
He is a man, baby!!!

Prof06
© 2008

35 One that will continue to stand
Tall
Trapped in the mind of another
To win this race of great proportion
He must not fall in such a way
40 That he gives up
Call him what you want
He will not front
Or fake the funk
In the mirror
45 I see him
I can't deny and shuck
This image
The mind that I am trapped in
Is my own
50 And the voice that I talk to
Is my conscience
Convicting me
For all that I have done wrong.

Over The Top

Some build from the ground up
Others take a more cerebral approach
In order to move mountains and to reach the
highest high
5   Takes courage, knowledge and strength
The Holy Spirit within provides
Taking into account our strengths and
weaknesses, my friend
We are only as near as we believe
10   Nothing is impossible
But first, you must dare to succeed
Discover what is hidden and rightfully yours
As simple as bending one knee
Commencing to accomplish your daily chores
15   God provides and sees us through
Questions will mount and there is still only One
That can instruct us on what to do
All of His plans are guaranteed
Be a blessing to someone else
20   To those in dire need
Now that you understand your purpose here
Symbolically bleed and sweat everyday
Paying homage to a Savior that did not have to
meet His demise
25   Our crosses are plenty to bear
Not comparing to His
But collectively a burden we share
If Calvary be the destination
Then gather your loins and the breastplate of
30   righteousness
And join me as I march to the top.

Prof06
© **2008**

Every time the window opens
A shadow of great proportions looms
To cast its ugly darkness about my hopes and
dreams
5   The mirror of talent is cracked and distorted
The shards of glass are about the floor
And I am running this race with bare feet
The fulfillment that I seek
Can be seen in the direction of my soul
10   Everyone wants to know if you have a plan
But no one wants to understand the intricacies of
it
So much talent, yet so misunderstood
If the truth hit you upside the head would you call
15   it a revelation or a headache?
Too many times stuck in a rut of increased despair
Work with me
Better yet, walk with me
On this journey of seclusion
20   I am sure that you do not have the heart or the
fortitude
To deal with the everyday letdowns and failures
My shoes are a size infinity
Which simply means that you cannot fill them
25   My unique talent, my one of a kind temperament
Creates a lasting impression as well as a lump of
fear
In the throats of all who think that they can hold
me down
30   The bitterness of my tone and the shakiness of my
step
May hinder me for a short while
But could never knock me down or out for a 10
count

Prof06
© **2008**

35   Because the Holy Spirit is too strong in me
You want me to smile
I would rather frown
I am in a place of pitch black solitude
If I asked, you would never join me
40   I fellowship with you through your good times and
your bad
It is a shame to say that I expected the same
When I curl up at night with my challenges and
my troubles
45   I am reliving the life of so many down in that
valley
I came back to the middle to get an understanding
or clarity
As I look back over my life
50   I am stunned at the accomplishments
Yet, I am overcome with feelings of pain
Concerning the many failures and no one to truly
pick me up
Can you relate to me?
55   Are you battered and bruised with all that you
have to go through
Ripped and torn between what is right and what is
wrong
What about choosing between what is right and
60   what is right?
Interesting conversation you would have with
yourself concerning these things
Mind warped and feelings damaged and numb
Knowing less about good and more about evil
65   The nights seem vicious and unbearable
The black knight is no longer a hero, but a foe
that chases you throughout the blackness of night
The angels have forsaken me

Prof06
© **2008**
110.

70

No longer protecting me from the snare of the
False one
My mind under a matter of striking proportions
Hands are no longer clean, but covered with
blood, dirt and unspoken violations
The soul of a believer can get weary

75

With my sword at hand
I pick up my tools to fight again once more
Who will join me?
Who will help me now?

80

Prof06
© **2008**

Amore

Wanting to disguise the pain
Of being broken into a million pieces
The sign "closed"
Reminds me of its nasty business
Clamped shut
Airtight
Not wanting to see the revealing signs of daylight
It shows too much
Exposes the reasons why to not "open" up
Countless wolves want to get to it
They think it is to be devoured
Forgetting that only a few
Just a few
Are destined to shower it with kindness
But with these eyes, they are hard to see
Understand that the wolves are dressed as sheep
They prey on the pacemaker
Plotting to steal it, batter it
Drain it's power to make it weak
For this reason
Staying on guard is an absolute must
It will be a long time
Before this heart can trust.

Prof06
© **2008**

Serious about asking me my intent?
I am a desperate man
Tired of the pain and lies
Seen through weary eyes
5   Of spiritual despair
Needing to give
To make another happy
Never been in my shoes
Wanting something so bad
10   But for someone else
Have you lost a loved one
Only the pain is so deep
You cannot even shed a tear?
Ever wanted to give a lady
15   Something she would cherish
And never forget
Free her of her pain
Fulfill a dream
One deferred for too long
20   It lives
An empty desire
A struggling soul
Not once being able to subconsciously
Make this woman smile
25   What she deserves
Tropical climate
Warm sands
Gorgeous people
African decent
30   In a distant land
The want for myself
But blessed enough
To give it to someone else
Not afraid to stand

Prof06
© **2008**

35
　　　　　　Not afraid to beg
　　　　　On a corner I stand
　　　　　With my spiritual cup
　　　　　　　　　In hand
　　　Waiting for a special gift
40
　　　　　　Unlike any other
　　　　I don't ask for myself
　　　　I ask for my mother.

It was created perfectly
Designed for my use
1% of it is brilliant
99% to remain dormant
5   If I could just tap into it
The rest of it, that is

With 1% use
How can I be 100% sure
10 About anything
What makes sense to me
May just about lose you
My vision is trained
Not on things worldly
15

Bangin' my head against the wall
Wanting and trying to understand
My underlying purpose
Dying a bit each day
20 My dreams are shackled and caged
Thoughts seem to betray me
Still living in the 1%

To open the mind
25 Is tougher than self expression
Or opening a book
Liberation is needed
Abstain from corruption
Beware of the rusted hook
30 Of Ignorance

More than gray matter
And white matter
More than tissue

Prof06
© 2008

35   And nerve endings
A muscle of knowledge
Given to create a world of...
Intelligent possibilities
A cloudy mind is devoid of..
40   Any sunshine
All in that 1%

Cerebrum, cerebellum, brainstem, cortex
The brain regulates more than bodily functions
45   Your entire life it directs
Shake it up
Meditate
Focus
Prayer
50   Help me
I am breaking out
I want more than 1%.

Jealousy and Envy Can Kill, Too

It's obvious when it creeps in
You don't have to know the commandments
To know the 10 things that
Unravel its mystery
5   Look in the eyes of those around you
That's one
Pay attention to key phrases and words
That seem to materialize out of nowhere
Negative in their intent and tone
10   That's two
Notice the broken fellowship
They don't know you now
And they blame you
That's three
15   When the smiles become crooked
No longer holding the same desires
Commitment is suddenly in short supply
You couldn't pay this person to be
REAL
20   With you anymore
That's four
You just get that feeling
That you are being clowned behind your back
That's discernment
25   And it's five
The absent phone calls
Not even a peep to see how life is treating you
People that I have known
For a blink of an eye
30   Have the concern to ask that
That's six
Finally, when you get a chance to come around
You learn that other people
Other friends seem to be closer

Prof06
© **2008**

117.

35   Wow, it seems that your place has been taken
That's seven
Other friends are mentioning to you things
That they thought that you knew
How cold is that?
40   That's eight
No Christmas cards
No birthday wishes
No please or thank yous
Just left wondering where it all went
45   That's nine
The fact that this is true
And many wish it wasn't written
Get over it
That's life
50   And that's ten.

Prof06
© 2008

Stepping into your realm
I had my guard down
I should have known that you fight dirty
Guard by my wayside
5   Caught up in your smile
I moved forward to get a better
Glimpse of your beauty
Time passes and feelings sway
Thinking that I could handle this meeting
10   Now on my knees to my dismay
Recollecting the decadent taste of
Sweet potato pie
Mixed with sinfully sweet honey
Thick on the lips
15   Sticky to the touch
Pretty Hot And Tempting
My d'fenses were down
How long has it been?
Since we said, "How Come?"
20   Now the plaster on the walls
Is peeling
The walls are sweating
The fire of love intensifies the night
Intoxication from the smells of ecstasy
25   Leave me drunk from anticipation
The lock on my heart has become
Nothing more than a twisty tie
Each word from your lips
Twists it in the opposite direction
30   Wanting to open the floodgates of my heart
You knew what you wanted
With the nature of a righteous woman
I could not begin to say, "No"
The distance has been our barrier

Prof06
© 2008

35   Two substances locked away
       Forbidden to exist together
    Knowing that our mixture creates an
       Explosion of possibilities
       You used to be afraid of me
40   What happened?
       Has the Sensual
       Cautious
       Lioness
       Decided to take her King?
45   Of your jungle I always ruled
       Not many snags there
  The land was always cut, edged and well groomed
       It has seen many wet days
       Because the vegetation and fruits
50   Are so juicy and sweet
    It is amazing what the presence of the right
       Lionheart can do
     In this trance I will stay until we touch
       Again for the first time.

55

Written in 2004

Father
Family Man
Educator
Mentor
Companion
Brother
Cousin
Friend
Man of God
Nephew
Son
Grandson
Alive

P

All the things that I am.

Whatever I missed, I am that, too.

As long as it is positive.

Flood Rush

The flood of fresh emotion
Committed to place a sour note on a new day
Larger purpose leading little candor
The smallest ones of which are in tow
5   The serenity of this day
Is drowned in the whines of
"mommy" and "daddy"
Just what were they thinking
What could be in store
10   The unknown can be frightening
It can be scary
Little puppy dog eyes
Filled with tears
The drama now, does not seem so mellow
15   The hugs turned into clings
And the smiles, are now last night's bitter dreams
How can one child last a school year
When they have drained a years worth of emotion
In just a few short moments
20   This is how I remember these faces
On the first day of school
This is how I remember you
When I was trying to hold back my own tears
My own fears and uncertainties
25   A Daddy of three worlds had multiplied into 11
My mathematics was fine
But suddenly Biology did not make any sense
A long time has past
But a certain fear still remains
30   To not screw up young minds
Is a narrow and tight line to walk
Teachers
Acrobats and gymnasts in our own right
We talk a good game

Prof06
© 2008

35   But in reality
A missed assignment
Poor handwriting
Lack of time management
Misplaced lesson plan
40   A runny nose
An absent mind
A push in line
Can leave us on the verge of going
Stark, raving mad
45   Teamwork is the key
We have it and we teach it to your children
It unlocks doors of compassion and understanding
It is a shame that the world does not really know
what it means to be a Christian
50   Now when I look into mature eyes
I see our leaders of tomorrow
Our Baracks, Martins, Malcolms, Sojourners,
Rosas, Medgars, Michaels, and Keys
Alicia that is because we already have musicians
55   and singers in our midst
I hear you
Parents
You talk about the information
The growth
60   The love
The commitment
The "oh no's and the no you don'ts"
And yes,
Mr. Watkins and I do have the nerve
65   You love Dads and Donuts
But we are Dad with Doctors, Dietitians, Dentists,
and Doctorate Achievers
In every field

Prof06
© 2008

They can't quit because we won't quit
70   Lord, don't get me started
Play back the tape in your minds
In our distant chapel lesson
We displayed Pastors, Scientists, Actresses,
Race Car Drivers, Doctors, Lawyers, Teachers
75   Etc. etc. etc.
And the list goes on.
The struggle that they brush off is not because
they do not embrace every test that the Lord gives
them
80   It is just that they will continue to push forward
and take life's lessons as God's way of purging
them and preparing them for what is to come
And nothing will stand in their way
Twinkle, twinkle little star
85   How I wonder what you are
Ask Girl Power
That's just not gonna cut it
They want to rhyme poems of substance
Read stories of hope and triumph
90   And when Jesus is talked about
Every ear and set of eyes are glued to His word
The Godstars are not just committed in name
But are committed in heart and spirit
They Kirk Franklined it into our hearts
95   George Huffed our minds
Because even in rain and snow
We all believed it to be a Brighter Day
With a touch of class
They gave us a touch of Coko
100   As they Clapped Their Hands
So by honoring us
You are honoring them

Prof06
© 2008

105

Because you are not happy with us
Unless you were first proud of them
To the parents and students
We give our gratitude
Thank you and
God bless you.

Put the needle on that wax
Play that jazz tune
The trumpet is smooth
Bass guitar strumming the cords
5   Of a delicate soul
The ivory twinkles with a sane madness
That captures a mind wandering afar
In comes the pippity pat boom boom
Of the drums
10   Character and coolness
Oozes from those sticks
That bang those beats

In steps the poet of the hour
15   Bohemian influence
With dashiki and tam
Soul Brother #1
Or Soul Sister Premiere
Poets of destiny
20   Formed out of rebellion
They are artists
With the constant flow
Tongues, lips and voices
Begin to paint a masterpiece
25   On intellectual canvas
Through the wonders of mental stimulation
And Imagination
Young, vibrant and clean
Militant in heart
30   Spiritual in soul
Embracing a culture
So black
So white
So tan

35   So brown
No matter
The colorful future
Is bright
Wetting each appetite
40   As verse and tune
Come to completion
It is not applause they are after
Just respect and satisfaction
Of producing and delivering
45   Their craft
To the masses.

The Black Knight is the one enemies fear
Playing to the crowd
Thunderous roars
Electric cheers
5 The prize at the end of this chess game
Is not the king
But my fare lady
The Queen
Can you blame a man
10 For risking it all
To achieve success
Between blacks and whites
On life's chessboard?
The beauty of the Queen is unmatched
15 C' she is from a ville-age
With many resources and much country
Humble beginnings
Destined for royalty
Her honey complexion
20 Coats a magnificent bone structure
With two sparkling gems for eyes
When she smiles
The court drops to its knees
Melting the toughest hearts
25 With her engaging personality
The heritage of her people
Runs deep within her
She is a Nubian pillar
Holding a myriad of things together
30 With the tips of her beautiful hands
Yes, her stature is known
Throughout the land

When the journey began

Prof06
© **2008**

35   A Pawn was I
Climbing an impossible ladder
Wishing upon stars
Blessing the moon of the sky
I was led to this place
40   Because destiny is mine
I then became a knight
Black armor
With an illustrious shine
I am the warrior that is respected
45   I defeat and defend against evil
To protect my fellow man
But there comes a time
When night falls
And the knight answers the call
50   Of his heart
For companionship
A warrior is dead inside
Without meaningful relationships
One in particular has caught his eye
55   He does not fight this battle for booty
But a slice of sweet potato pie
The king can keep his riches
This knight just wants a diamond
Victory means that a Queen will be saved
60   Sword drawn and ready
Will this be the day?

Prof06
© **2008**

The Blues
The Wintertime Blues
Sleepless nights
The heat is too high
5   Why can't I find a little creavice
To climb into
To just get a little sleep
My mind is racing
The Cuervo Black didn't help
10   Beads of sweat
The sheets are soaked
Whatever happened to peaceful tranquility
It somehow got swallowed up in the dark
Loneliness creeps in
15   The feeling is all too familiar
Dank and musty
Tossing and turning
Maybe a shower would be in order
Staying awake seems ok
20   Nothing to watch
But Freddy's Nightmares
That won't go away
The Bible sits near
Seemingly too far out of reach
25   On a nightstand
Hello, hello
Do you see the dilemma?
It is cold outside
An oven here
30   Inside
No window pane to crack
Because the problems are more
Than just a temperature adjustment

Prof06
© **2008**

35 Muscles are sore and aching
Jack Johnson and Tyson are to blame
They tossed my emotions like a simmering
sausage
In and out of the ring
40 To the jeers of a demonly crowd
They don't seem to want to share my fate
Fore theirs has already been sealed
I am the new company that they are only
Too welcomed
45 To usher in
Hello, hello
I cannot find the sun
Has anyone seen him
I am dying to have its light rise
50 On my crumbling and hysterical emotional state
Black
Blackness
Complete and total blackness
You can see the rain in the dark
55 You can only feel its touch
The wetness licks your wounds
Only sooner or later
To attempt to drown you
Where is the light?
60 The switch is non existence
Or just out of reach like that Bible
The knocking inside of my mind get louder
To a fever pitch
I am stuck in some heavy metal state
65 I can hear
I don't understand the words
But the motions are not of this world

Prof06
© 2008

132.

Hello, hello
70   The door cracks
A ray of light pierces that darkness
Like unfiltered hope
I reach of it
But again, it is too far away!
75   A hand is near
I am jerked upward
More light
Bright light
I am blinded
80   But the sounds that I hear
Are familiar
And filled with love
Now I have to figure out
Whether I am dead or alive
85   Hello, hello
Or is it goodbye?

Acknowledgements to the Faithful

The ultimate thank you goes to my Lord and Savior Jesus Christ! I am glad to be in communion with you and look forward to the day in which I can join you in sitting with Our Father in heaven. I honor my parents for giving me a chance at life. It truly took two to make this one. Mom, I thank you for your undying support of my efforts in all areas of my life. It has really been a journey thus far. Praise the Lord for my wonderful sisters. I continue to set the bar for you. Not out of competition, but out of love. Paving the way is no easy task, but something that has to be done to make life more complete for us all. My brothers are vital for my development as a man. I am able to use my older brother as a role model and my younger brother as a reminder of some of the things that I have come through. Thank you to you both. There is nothing like a Grandmother's love. She still continues to believe in me and to show her support. It goes without saying that I appreciate all of her love and prayers. My aunts have withstood the test of time and have always come through with support. I can't express my gratitude enough. This one is for you Granddad! We all love and miss you, GD/DC. A rock is hard to find in a family. Thanks to all of my cousins. I know your heart and your commitment to my works. We miss each other a lot, but the love is always felt. To my friends and extended family members, what can I say? You guys have been the spokes to my wheels for so long. I can't name each and every one of you, but you all know how I feel about you and the special place that you have in my heart of hearts. Many of you sit in the inner chamber right where Jesus sits on the throne of my heart. Pastor, I appreciate you and the

Prof06
© 2008

134.

Acknowledgements to the Faithful

Pleasant Grove Family. We have been through a lot together, but your support of me says volumes as to the type of church that we have and how we serve others. You have always been there for me in my time of need. Thanks be unto God for you.

A round of applause for my students is in order. They have kept me lifted for at least 3 years! They have cared for me in ways that have touched my soul. You guys are family to me. I love you like my own 3 Treasures. I thank the Lord for your parents because you are extensions of them and they are the leaders who have made my life easier as well. Many of you guys have become good friends and I cherish that as well. Thank you. To my children, Daddy has done it once again! I hope that you are proud. I love you guys so much and you have my heart and my soul with you always. You all have been inspirations beyond belief. Thank you Brittany, Zyon, and Autumn for keeping your Dad in your prayers and loving me unconditionally. You have given me all that a father could ask for.

Special thanks to Rita B. You have had a Brother's back for as long as I can remember. This project has your stamp of approval and you have been very instrumental in aiding its production. My love and heart go to you. Every person needs a support system and you have done the job of 10 people, at least. Please keep doing God's will for your life and in the lives of others. To my best friend of almost 15 years, Antoinette B., I am glad that you helped to make this project special. Your support was and always will be needed. Thanks a million! If I missed

Prof06
© 2008

Acknowledgements to the Faithful

you, don't panic. I did not omit you on purpose.
Besides, I will be writing books for many, many years
and you have plenty of time to make an impact and
to influence my life.

"If you think that you can achieve greatness with ease, then wait a while...opposition is surely on its way. When it begins, if you can find your way through the darkness, then the light is a well deserved conclusion."

--Jumanne Bradford inspired by Langston Hughes

Don't forget to check out the other two titles that are available, by visiting www.profxshonworks.biz Thank you and God bless you.